THE WORLD OF
NASCAR

RACE WEEK:
Seven Crazy Days

By Stephen Timblin

The
**Child's
World**®
www.childsworld.com

www.childsworld.com

Published in the United States of America by
The Child's World®
1980 Lookout Drive • Mankato, MN 56003-1705
800-599-READ • www.childsworld.com

ACKNOWLEDGMENTS

The Child's World®:
Mary Berendes, Publishing Director

Produced by Shoreline Publishing Group LLC
President / Editorial Director: James Buckley, Jr.
Designer: Tom Carling, carlingdesign.com
Assistant Editor: Jim Gigliotti

Photo Credits:
Cover: Joe Robbins
Interior: AP/Wide World: 4, 12, 15, 21;
Getty Images: 6; Joe Robbins: 1, 2, 8, 11,
16, 18, 22, 24, 27, 28

**LIBRARY OF CONGRESS
CATALOGING-IN-PUBLICATION DATA**

Timblin, Stephen.
  Race week : seven crazy days / by Stephen
Timblin.
     p. cm. — (The world of NASCAR)
  Includes bibliographical references and index.
  ISBN 978-1-60253-079-9 (library bound : alk.
paper)
  1. Stock car racing—United States—Juvenile
literature. 2. NASCAR (Association)—Juvenile
literature. I. Title. II. Series.

  GV1029.9.S74T56 2008
  796.72—dc22

                    2007049081

Contents

[OPPOSITE]
*It's just about time to take the track and
race! How did these cars prepare for this
moment? Let's find out.*

From Finish to Start

THE CHECKERED FLAG WAVES AS A THUNDERING
line of race cars speeds across the finish line. Another
grueling NASCAR Sprint Cup race has ended. The crowd
roars its approval under the hot sun, and your favorite
driver has won the day.

After the celebrations and post-race interviews wrap
up, you can turn off the TV. Or, if you're lucky enough to
be at the race, it's time to head back to the parking lot
for the drive home. The driver and his crew, however,
don't have the luxury of taking a break. Before the car's
engine has even has a chance to cool down, it's already
time to get back to work.

From the beginning of February through the end
of October, the life of a NASCAR driver and his crew is
one giant cycle. The driver is the leader of the pack, and
nearly every hour of his week is planned ahead of time.

Behind every driver is a supporting cast that can
number in the hundreds, from mechanics and engineers
to truck drivers and fitness experts. Week after week, your
favorite NASCAR driver shows up on race day in a car so
shiny you'd think it just rolled out of the factory. It is the
result of incredibly hard work by the entire team.

Keep reading to find out what that team does from
the minute one race ends to the start of the next.

[OPPOSITE]
*The chase to the
checkered flag begins
long before the green
flag is dropped to
start the race.*

Great Race— Now Do It Again!

FOOTBALL COACHES ARE KNOWN FOR TELLING their teams that playing in a game is the easy part— practice is where all the important work is done.

The same can be said about racing in NASCAR. When a race ends, the driver and his team are exhausted. They'd love to relax with their families or even hit the hot tub. But there isn't any time for that.

For starters, right after a race ends the top five finishers—along with a few other cars picked at random— have to go through a post-race **inspection**. This is the toughest inspection that NASCAR does, as officials want to make sure the cars weren't tampered with since the pre-race inspection. Along with the easy stuff, like re-checking the car's height and weight, the inspectors order what they call a "tear-down." Inspectors can ask to have the engines, **suspension systems**, and more completely

[OPPOSITE]
Jeff Gordon tries to cool down after a hard day at the track. He doesn't have much time to rest, though, before the weekly cycle starts up again.

taken apart, and the race team is required to help. Competing teams can watch this tear-down if they want to. "It gives them peace of mind knowing that everything was legal," says Mike Ford, the crew chief that keeps Denny Hamlin's No. 11 Chevrolet purring. "If things were done behind closed doors, it would always lead to questions about what happened back there."

After the post-race inspection is completed, it's time to load the truck. A NASCAR transporter truck, called a hauler, is the most organized vehicle you'll ever see.

These massive 18-wheel trucks, known as "haulers," hit the road hours after the race is over. They are filled to the brim with a race team's gear.

Wheel-Life Celebrities

If you feel like you're not getting enough attention lately, maybe you should drive a NASCAR hauler. These massive trucks, colorfully decorated with the decals of their race teams, attract plenty of stares and honks as they cruise down America's interstate highways. People in passing cars wave and take pictures. Some call on the **CB radio** to offer congratulations—or the opposite if they're not fans of the hauler's racing team! So many people react to the trucks, in fact, that the long-haul drivers' bring along hats and glossy photos of the car or driver to be given out to appreciative fans—or curious highway patrolmen!

Back in NASCAR's early days, a hauler was just a van with a race car on a trailer behind it, and the driver was often the race driver himself. Nowadays, these haulers are massive, 18-wheel tractor-trailers worth $300,000 each. And that's peanuts compared to the cost of the equipment inside the trucks, which can be worth as much as $1.5 million.

Why so much? It's because the trucks hold two race cars (a primary and a backup), along with all the equipment and tools used in the pit and the speedway garage. The trucks also act as a command center, where the team can talk over strategies in private. So they have a lounge area that is stocked with a TV, computer, and a snack-filled kitchen.

By the time a hauler is fully loaded, there is hardly any unused space. After loading the hauler, most of the crew get cleaned up and head to the airport. But the truck drivers' work is just starting. If it's a short drive to the team garage, one driver will handle the job. If getting back hime is a long haul—say, Texas to North Carolina—two drivers will share the work, so that nobody gets sleepy behind the wheel.

This is no joyride for the drivers. "When I drive the transporter, I don't play the stereo, and my hands are at 10 and 2," says Robby Maschhaupt, a hauler for Robby Gordon Motorsports (he means that he keeps his hands on the steering wheel in proper driving position). "I'm really paying attention. It takes a lot to drive one of these and you have to keep a safety zone around you at all times."

For some race team members, Monday means a little downtime—maybe their only time off all week. The men in the haulers get to catch up on sleep. If he's lucky, the race driver, drained from Sunday's competition, will get a day off to collect his thoughts. Most of the mechanics get right to work, though.

A big crew of race team members is usually unloading the truck by 7 A.M. They give the thrashed race car a quick **debriefing** to see what changed after the start of the race. Any dents to fix? Any problems with the rear

In the 1950s, team owner Carl Kiekhaefer was the first man to transport his cars to the track by truck or van. Before that, drivers simply got behind the wheel and drove the cars there themselves!

wing? It all gets checked out. The next priority is to get the engine into the engine shop. By Monday afternoon, Sunday's car is a skeleton, stripped down to its bare bones. Meanwhile, the crew chief and his engineers do a post-race summary. They talk about what went right—and wrong—in Sunday's race, and how they can improve the next weekend. From one Sunday to the next, a race car might be almost totally rebuilt from the tires up.

Communication is the key between a crew chief and driver. Here, car No. 20 crew chief Greg Zipadelli talks things over with driver Tony Stewart.

Life in the Beehive

AS THE WEEK MOVES ON, THE WORK GETS

more intense and a NASCAR race team might be working on as many as a half-dozen cars. They'll be focusing on that week's ride, of course, and cars for the next few races after that.

A huge part of the equation is testing. Teams are permitted a limited amount of testing days at tracks running Sprint Cup events, and time spent driving at upcoming tracks is extremely precious. Because they can't spend all their time at tracks, teams will also do **wind tunnel** tests, using computer sensors to measure things such as air flow around the car and how much the machine vibrates. "Testing is where you get a lot of your chemistry between driver and crew chief, but it's about engineers, too," says Eddie Wood, a longtime crew chief and co-owner of the Wood Brothers Racing team. "Test is an engineer's middle name."

In analyzing a car, the team spends much of its time studying the **chassis** setup and how it affects aerodynamics. A NASCAR team has many types of springs and shocks available to make adjustments. And every track is a little different, whether because of the surface or the bank of the curves. The key is to match the right equipment to the right track.

[OPPOSITE]
All week long, teams study their cars inside and out. The car shown here was from an event that let fans see what the inside of a NASCAR racer looks like.

13

Stock-car mechanics might be fun-loving guys, but with all of this testing and technology involved a NASCAR garage is a pretty serious place. There isn't a lot of goofing off. It's almost like a hive full of busy worker bees. And Monday through Thursday, from 7:00 A.M. until darkness falls, it's pretty much buzzing with the sounds of air guns and air wrenches.

Even though he might not be the one changing the tires, the busiest bee in the hive is the driver. If the team is conducting tests at an upcoming racetrack, the driver must be there to provide **feedback**. These tests can last as long as a race, meaning a driver has to be ready to

Hearts of Gold

Jeff Gordon, one of NASCAR's top drivers for more than a decade, averages an incredible 300 **sponsor** appearances a year. Add all the hours spent racing and testing, and who could blame him for using the rest of his spare time to hit the beach? Instead, the man behind the No. 24 Chevy helps run the Jeff Gordon Foundation, a charity that funds children's hospitals. "You want to help everyone, but that's impossible," Gordon explains. "You have to focus on what is closest to your heart." The foundation is a huge commitment, eating up plenty of Gordon's time and effort—but he's not the only driver with a heart of gold. "Nearly every driver has a foundation to support a cause he believes in, and we all support each other whenever we can," says Gordon. "It's one of the things I love about this sport."

run hundreds of grueling laps during midweek practice sessions between races.

The race car, however, is far from the driver's only task during the week. NASCAR is a huge and expensive business, and teams can't survive without sponsors. The main sponsor of a Sprint Cup series car pays an average of $10 million each year, and secondary sponsors can

pay several million dollars as well. These companies expect more than just their **logos** plastered on the race cars and uniforms for all that money. So during the racing season, a driver's midweek schedule is loaded with autograph signings, factory visits, banquets, photo shoots, interviews, and even TV commercial shoots, all done to please the sponsors.

If that sounds to you like drivers don't get much time off, you're right. "The career span for a race car driver is going to shorten up tremendously over the next 10 to 15 years, I think," says superstar driver Dale Earnhardt Jr., describing the hectic lifestyle that modern-day NASCAR drivers live. "All the commitments and things that we're going through, the things that we are involved in on and off the track, I think it's going to take its toll."

Back at the garage, the primary car is in final prep by Thursday morning. Workers tape the front end and wax the car. By late afternoon, the team will have finished any test runs, and will have a head start on two future races. Most important, it will have this Sunday's car in working order. All that's left is to get the beast to the track.

The bright colors and sponsor logos on a NASCAR car are usually giant stickers that fit over the car. Not Jeff Gordon's No. 24 car, though. It's painted, because his sponsor is a paint company!

Inspect and Perfect

DAYTONA. TALLADEGA. BRISTOL. RACING FANS

descend upon these famous racetracks from all over the country when NASCAR's traveling motor sports show is in town. And so do the race teams.

Thursday is a travel day, with teams either driving or flying to the racetrack in the evening. The driver doesn't drive his race car there, of course, but instead shows up to find a motor home waiting for him and his family. Drivers used to stay in nearby hotels, but with so many weekends spent racing they realized it made more sense to stay at the track. But don't feel bad for the drivers. Loaded with all the comforts of home, these high-class motor homes blow away any hotel room with the likes of flat-screen TVs, computer hookups, leather couches, and state-of-the-art kitchens.

The weekend kicks off early on Friday with the first of up to five official inspections. Each team is expected to show up by 7:00 A.M. so inspectors can check that everything meets the strict guidelines outlined in NASCAR's 92-page rule book. The officials want to make sure the car's major **components** all meet the standard regulations so that no team has an unfair advantage. This initial inspection lasts several hours, and teams line up in order of their drivers' point totals. The leaders get to go

[OPPOSITE]
Race inspections are important—they let racers, fans, and the media know that every team is playing by the same rules.

19

first; the lower-ranked drivers have to wait a long time. Officials enter the garage to examine the car's carburetor and fuel cell—a fancy term for the gas tank—to make sure it holds the proper amount of gas (18 gallons; 68 liters) and not a drop more. They also weigh the car, which has to tip the scales to at least 3,400 pounds (1,542 kg) without a driver, and measure the car's height to ensure it's at least 51 inches (130 cm) tall. An inspector may allow the team to fix minor issues right then. But if a car fails any part of the inspection, the team must make the required changes and go through the process again.

[OPPOSITE]
Qualifying runs are when NASCAR drivers can let it all hang out.

Once a car passes the initial inspection, it's time for practice laps. Teams practice for two hours, and after that comes more tinkering. The crew might change a shock absorber or two or adjust the timing. And then . . . another inspection. If an illegal part is found during this or any other inspection, it is taken away and put on display for all the other teams to view; the team could also face stiff fines and even be banned from several races.

By about 3 P.M. on Friday, it's time for **qualifying**. This is when drivers take turns steering their cars around the track at the highest speeds possible to determine their starting position in Sunday's race. The fastest qualifiers get to start at the head of the pack. The quickest car of all is on the pole, in front and to the inside. Qualifying order is based on a random draw. If a

driver has an early draw, he might need to quit practice early to get through inspection.

All teams know that part of race week is waiting through the necessary inspections.

The main goal of qualifying is to run a fast lap, of course, but the team is also looking closely at how the car performs. After qualifying, the top five cars go through yet another inspection. And if you think the team that

Hot Wheels

One thing racing teams don't have to lug to each track are tires. That's because NASCAR requires everyone to use the same company's tires. The company makes 18 different types of tires to match the changing conditions at different speedways. Of course, these aren't the same tires that your family's car uses. Not only are they wider than regular tires, but they also don't have any **treads**—there's no snow or mud on the tracks to worry about, after all.

While a regular set of tires lasts about 50,000 miles (80,467 km), these hot wheels burn out after only 150 miles (241 km). Depending on the length of a race and the track's surface, each team will go through 9 to 14 sets of tires. That means up to 2,000 tires can be used by all the cars combined in a single race!

Once they get to the tracks, teams carefully inspect and organize their stock of tires. Each tire is carefully measured and tested so they can pick only the very best for their driver's car. Then, teams will use some tires in qualifying and save some for the race.

wins the **pole position** gets a break, think again. That team actually has to completely tear down its car's engine so NASCAR officials can re-check all the parts.

By Friday evening, the driver and his team have a clear plan for the weekend. But that doesn't mean everyone gets a peaceful sleep that night. The teammates usually wake up early on Saturday morning with their heads full of strategies.

The Final Countdown

AT 7:00 A.M. SATURDAY MORNING, WHEN KIDS are crawling out of bed to watch cartoons and many parents are trying to hide under the pillows, NASCAR teams are already at the track.

There are generally two practice sessions on Saturday. The mechanics use them to make adjustments to the car's "setup." That's the term NASCAR gearheads use for how a car's tires, shocks, and balance are lined up for each track. The final hour of practice is known as "Happy Hour," and it's a wild 60 minutes filled with last-second tweaks and talks. Before turning out the shop lights, the team installs a new, unscratched windshield and cleans up the garage area.

Finally, the big day arrives. You know how we keep talking about showing up for work at 7:00 A.M.? That's the best-case **scenario** for Sunday morning. If the race is at

[OPPOSITE]
At the end of a long week, it's finally time to get behind the wheel. The special heel pads that Kasey Kahne is putting on here will protect his feet from the high heat of the engine and the pedals.

a superspeedway such as Daytona or Talladega, NASCAR insists on restrictor plates to keep top speeds down and drivers safe. This makes the inspections take longer. So if it's a restrictor-plate race, the officials want teams on-site at the cruel hour of 4:00 A.M. Otherwise, garage gates open at 7:00.

As race time approaches, the mechanics work on putting every tool and spare part in the pit area within arm's reach in case it's needed during a pit stop. The driver doesn't get time to relax, either, as on race mornings he has another sponsor meeting. Known as hospitality, this is when drivers dress up nice to meet and greet friends of their sponsors. The drivers answer questions and sign autographs—all while trying to keep their minds focused on the big race ahead.

Three hours before the green flag, the crew pushes the car onto pit road. The fans in the stands already go crazy at the sight. The driver and crew chief then head off to the mandatory drivers' meeting to discuss any final rules or issues. Being on time is vital; drivers who show up late get moved to the last-place spot in the starting lineup, regardless of where they qualified.

Before firing up the engines for "The Show" (which is what teams call the race), drivers are introduced one-by-one to a sea of screaming fans. The crew chief then might have time to give the driver a last pep talk, but

The drivers' meeting is the only time that all the teams' drivers and crew chiefs are together. Sometimes, the discussions among rivals can get pretty lively!

there isn't really a whole lot to say at this point. The two men have already had their talks about strategy during the week.

And for the drivers, their long list of responsibilities throughout the week finally shrinks to just one thing: racing! When Dale Earnhardt Jr., puts on his helmet, is buckled into his No. 88 car, and grabs the wheel, his

Before each race, the drivers are introduced to the crowd. They circle the entire track so all the fans can get a good look at them before the helmets go on!

mind clears for the first time all week. "When you're driving and concentrating on that race car, there's really nothing else to think about," says Junior. "There's not room for anything else."

And after a week of long hours and unending toil, getting to clear your mind to focus on an afternoon of hard racing seems like a great break.

Work It Out!

After their busy weeks, most drivers can't wait to start racing. But that doesn't mean that they have an easy task ahead of them. It takes serious **stamina** to muscle a land rocket speeding up to 200 miles (322 km) per hour around a track for four hours. And temperatures in a race car can be as high as 130 degrees F (54 degrees C), meaning drivers sweat off as much as 10 pounds (5 kg) during a race! All that means that just like hoops heroes, gridiron greats, and other professional athletes, NASCAR's stars have to stay in great shape if they want to succeed. That's why many drivers, including Jimmie Johnson, Carl Edwards, and Dale Jarrett, are well-known gym rats.

"I lift weights and run or bike Monday through Friday, then Saturday do an additional day of running or riding," says Jarrett, who has won more than 30 NASCAR Cup races.

Along with improving stamina, hard-charging driver Casey Mears brings up another important reason for working out that other professional athletes don't have to worry about: "Being healthy and in shape not only helps you with endurance and strength, but also if you get in a bad accident your body can handle the impact better."

Glossary

CB radio a radio system people use to talk to each other over short distances ("CB" is short for "Citizens' Band")

chassis the steel framework of a car

components connected parts that make up a whole

debriefing asking questions to gain knowledge about something

feedback opinions and thoughts shared to improve something

inspection to examine something or to look at it very closely

logos a symbol that represents a company or a team

pole position the best starting spot—the inside of the front row

qualifying earning a spot in the finals of an event

rivals people who compete against each other in a contest

scenario a possible chain of events

sponsor a company that pays an athlete or team to promote its products

stamina staying power and endurance

suspension systems the parts of a car that let the driver handle it, such as steering and shock absorbers

treads the pattern of grooves and notches found on a tire, used to channel away rain, mud, and snow

wind tunnel a tunnel-like room with forced air from fans; people use wind tunnels to study how air flows around an object

Find Out More

BOOKS

Eyewitness NASCAR
By James Buckley, Jr.
DK Publishing, 2005
This photo-filled book takes you inside the world of NASCAR. See close-up pictures of engines and other gear, meet the heroes of the sport, and see more photos of pit-stop and racing action.

NASCAR at the Track
By Mike Kennedy and Mark Stewart
Lerner Publishing, 2007
This book takes a close-up look at various NASCAR tracks, showing how they're designed, built, and how drivers attack each type of track.

NASCAR For Dummies
By Mark Martin and Beth Tuschak
Wiley Publishing, Inc., 2005
Martin, the veteran NASCAR driver, fills readers in on the basics of NASCAR . . . and a whole lot more.

NASCAR Record & Fact Book
Sporting News Books, 2008
This handy reference source is loaded with facts and figures about current drivers and NASCAR history.

Pit Pass
By Bob Woods
Readers' Digest Children's Publishing, 2005
Take an "inside" look at NASCAR tracks, drivers, cars, and gear.

WEB SITES

Visit our Web site for lots of links about NASCAR:
www.childsworld.com/links

Note to Parents, Teachers, and Librarians: We routinely check our Web links to make sure they're safe, active sites—so encourage your readers to check them out!

Index

ABOUT THE AUTHOR

Stephen Timblin is a longtime writer and an all-around sports nut. He has interviewed everyone from Tony Hawk to Tony Stewart and still hopes to one day become a pro snowboarder. Stephen lives in the car capital of the country—Detroit, Michigan.